end

MW01242512

"*The Family Letter* is a proven method of generational transformation. After hearing Debi Ronca speak on the concept of family letters several years ago, I decided to implement that concept in my own family. Not only do we look forward to hearing each other's hearts as well as the words of encouragement and affirmation through the letters, I can honestly say it redefined the culture in our home. I look forward to sharing this tradition with our daughters' future husbands and our grandchildren."

Laura Bradshaw
President of Journey U

"*The Family Letter* is an amazing tool to help you grow closer with your loved ones. Sometimes it's hard to know where or how to start changing the tone within your home and family and Debi Ronca has made it so simple. When you put these strategies into practice, you will be amazed at the growth, warmth, appreciation and honor that occurs. No matter where you are at in life, you can begin this journey today."

Charity Bradshaw
Author | Business Coach

the family letter

HOW TO INTENTIONALLY
DEVELOP A CULTURE
OF HONOR, ENCOURAGEMENT
& VALUE WITH YOUR LOVED ONES

DEBI RONCA

LIFEWISE BOOKS

the family letter
How to Intentionally Develop a Culture of Honor, Encouragement & Value with Your Loved Ones
DEBI RONCA

Published by:

⚓ LIFEWISE BOOKS

PO BOX 1072
Pinehurst, TX 77362
LifeWiseBooks.com

Cover Design and Interior Layout | Yvonne Parks | PearCreative.ca

To contact the author | DebiRonca.com

ISBN (Print): 978-1-947279-56-8
ISBN (Ebook): 978-1-947279-57-5

dedication

Throughout the years, you have all been a part of this sacred tradition that took place around our dining room table. Years of laughter, shared tears and encouragement still ring true as we gather to celebrate each other's lives. Thank you for holding this tradition close to your heart, for always wanting to write your letters, and for passing the tradition on to the next generation where your children, my grandchildren, will carry the torch.

special tribute

I would like to thank my husband, Michael, for his love and
support to follow my dreams. Your unconditional love and
encouragement over the years have allowed me to follow my
heart and the calling on my life. Without you, my love, none
of this would be possible. I have loved raising our children with
you, and now we are reaping together the joy filled season of
being Nana and Papi. More memories to be made with you, the
love of my life.

special acknowledgement

Thank you, Melody Barker and Charity Bradshaw, for your
wisdom, expertise and inspiration to spur me over the finish
line to the completion of my first book. It has been a wonderful
experience working with you, and I am honored that you both
have chosen to adopt "The Family Letter" tradition within your
own family. Write on!

table of contents

chapter one

A NEW MINDSET

UNDERSTANDING THE WHY

Have you ever stopped to wonder what it would be like to hear what your loved ones really felt about you? Does this thought send chills up your spine, or does it stir up a longing inside of you? Imagine how you would feel if you knew their innermost thoughts about your character, your personality, and all the things that makes you, you. The truth is that everyone, regardless of age, sex or cultural background, has the deep desire to be encouraged, to be recognized and to be inspired by the thoughts of others towards them. Honestly, who would not want to experience this empowerment?

The power of thoughtful intentional words literally breathes life into us and allows us to soar with confidence in the direction of our goals and the courage to believe and embrace the purposes of God in our lives. Words have power. Proverbs 18:21*a* NAS says, *"Death and life are in the power of the tongue."* It is a sobering thought to know that our words have that much influence or power. They are considered potent in one way or the other.

> Many of us think our words don't offer enough value to impact another person.

I sometimes wonder why we adopt this mindset. Maybe we think our words have no power connected to them. Maybe we say to ourselves, "What difference would it make?" Or do we think we are being too emotional and don't want to appear foolish if we share how we really feel?

While these all could be possible reasons why we hold back, this line of thinking winds up holding us hostage. It is as if our mouths have been sealed with our words trapped in our heart and mind, never released to our loved ones who desperately need to hear how we feel. The mindset of believing our words don't carry value needs to be transformed. It's time to adjust our thinking and begin to understand this is more than some nice words or even fluff. Our words impart life, encouragement and instill legacy and value to those who are the fortunate recipients.

Another issue could be our busy schedules. We may have an encouraging thought or personal feeling about someone, and have the intention of telling them, but the fast pace of life swoops in and steals the moment. We don't make time to follow through and consequently forget. We end up never conveying these valuable feelings to our family or our friends. The consequence? We live our lives void of affirmation, acceptance and inspiration from loved ones and those we consider close from our inner circles.

LOST IN INTENTIONS

These unspoken words, literally life-givers to the soul, are held captive and lost in the realm of good intentions. The fact that today's modes of communication are more impersonal is another hurdle we need to conquer. Texting and e-mails are crammed with overly simplified emoji's that have become the method of conveying our most basic feelings and emotions. Happy, sad, angry, dancing, you name it, and you can even purchase more to have an arsenal ready to use when you "speak" to your friends.

How many of us now have a Bitmoji that looks like us? We use them to add that seemingly personal touch to our text messages. How convenient. Lots of fun. Without us realizing it, the most powerful and intimate way of communicating has slowly eroded. It has been replaced by a method that has removed what has always been the original intent– the personal connection.

Let me encourage you with some good news. It is never too late to become intentional with your words regardless of the dynamics or ages within your family or close relationships. Don't let the past, or the circumstances you find yourself in right now, deter you or make you feel that this is impossible, or that it won't really matter. In all honesty, your words do matter and will make a difference. With God's help, they will pierce the darkness that surrounds your most difficult relationships while establishing deeper roots in your already healthy ones. So, if your heart desires to bring life to and strengthen the bonds in your relationships, you are now positioned to step into a new way of thinking and learn a new process.

A FRESH START

My heart in writing this book is to show you a few simple, yet profound insights and strategies to help you implement using the power of words with your loved ones. This can be a fresh start, the beginning of a new mindset and way of sharing your feelings. Writing your feelings out for someone is a priceless gift that will literally touch people's hearts, bring healing to relationships and create memories that will last a lifetime. You can create and even change the culture in your home yielding fruit that will last for generations. Are you ready?

Within the pages of this book, you will learn how to generate and produce change that will take your most valued relationships to a higher and deeper level. The power of words is fundamental to life. So, let's journey together and discover how we can begin this simple yet powerful practice.

chapter two

THE GENESIS

In the early years of our marriage, my husband and I discussed over and over how we wanted the culture of our home to be different from the ones we grew up in. We both had loving parents, but they came from a generation that was not comfortable sharing how they felt. Their emotions were almost a private thing for them. We knew they loved us, but they had a hard time expressing their emotions in everyday life.

What we both would have given to hear our parents' *tender* loving words. Words spoken by a parent that just melts your heart and makes you feel so valuable and loved.

It seems as though the generation that came before us did not understand the importance of encouragement and affirmation. They may have thought those words, but the feelings were not personally conveyed. This could be a huge part of the way they were raised themselves. For many from that generation, love was demonstrated by what they did to provide for their children. We can say our parents truly did so much for us and were great providers for what we needed.

For our parents, their heart-felt focus was to make sure we had a nice home to live in, food on the table, a good education and some fun vacations along the way. This, by the way, was wonderful. We both have fond memories of those times. These were our basic needs (with some extra thrown in) and they met them to the best of their ability. They loved us in their own way and for that we honor our parents and shower them with the highest respect. We saw their sacrifice and hard work to provide all they did and we are beyond grateful. We love and bless them! Our heart in moving forward was to build on the foundation our parents lovingly gave us and make an even stronger one for our children.

THE GAP

What was missing was something our hearts longed for—words of affirmation, praise and acceptance. Having this gap in our emotional tank simply caused us both to acknowledge that we wanted to add this into the mix of how we raised and loved our children. We did not want them to grow up with that same longing of the soul. We wanted our relationships to be different and impactful.

Bearing this thought in mind, we decided the best way that we could foster closer relationships and true affection in our home was to be intentional in sharing words of life and affirmation to each other and to our children. We knew if we modeled it to them as they were growing up, they would naturally begin to follow our footsteps. As a result of our commitment, our children grew up being hugged and told how much they were loved. Their God-given talents were recognized and celebrated, and we encouraged them to grow in strength, purpose and tenderness of heart.

THEIR OWN STRUGGLE

As the years went by, we realized that even though as parents we were affirming our children, they struggled to do the same for their siblings. What was the problem? "Why the struggle?", we thought. Our curiosity drove us to ask our children where the disconnect was between receiving it themselves and then being able to impart it to each other.

Their honesty and transparency gave us the clarity we needed and the key to unlock the problem. We discovered their fear of not knowing what to say or even how to say it. They felt unsure and ill-equipped. After all, they were only five and seven years old at the time.

> We sometimes forget that communication skills need to be taught, nurtured and developed.

Now that we had identified the issues, the question shifted to how to solve it and free our children to release their feelings and emotions in a friendly and safe way. We revisited our game plan. "What is our goal?" we asked ourselves. Our goal was to teach them how to speak words of life to each other and how to develop the power of encouragement. This encouragement wasn't only meant to be vertical from parent to child, it was also supposed to be horizontal, child to child. It could be poured out to each member of our family from each member of our family.

THE ANSWER

We knew our goal and purpose, but now it was the method that eluded us. We took some time to think about it, sharing ideas that we thought would work, and then it came loud and clear. This could all be done through the power of a written letter. "A written letter?", you might ask. "How can that be the catalyst for the breakthrough?" Follow me through the next chapters and I will share with you the most powerful tool in our family, the *Family Letter*.

chapter three

RULES OF ENGAGEMENT

The simple act of writing a letter became the greatest platform we used to establish the culture of love and honor in our home. It was a game changer on every level. Our family decided that this letter was to be written each year on the birthday of each family member. Since birthdays are typically times of celebration, we felt this would be the perfect day to be told what others feel about you and how they celebrate your life.

To make it easy, we established "rules for writing". The rules were simple. In fact, having guidelines really frees up the person to pen their thoughts. It serves to gives ideas, themes and by establishing a procedure, it actually helps the words flow a little easier than if you had to come up with your own plan or format.

THE CRITERIA

Here are the criteria we followed when writing the Family Letter:

- Encourage the recipient by sharing what good things you see in them. Things like their sense of humor, compassion, their desire to help others, etc.

- Encourage them in the gifts and talents that you see in them.

- Share with them how you specifically love them and why, and how they have impacted your life.

- If they have gone through a hard time, encourage them on how you have seen them walk through their difficulty.

- Share with them God's perspective on their trial and give them hope.

- Celebrate and recognize any accomplishments they may have experienced and share your excitement in how the Lord has blessed them and is using them in their place in life. This could be school, business, at home, etc.

- Share on how the Lord can use them in future endeavors as they grow into different seasons of life. Share scriptures, or any prophetic words you have that will encourage and inspire.

These guidelines enable the one writing the letter to not only reflect on the life of the recipient but also have a focus so as to not feel lost or overwhelmed. Reflection is powerful. It provides the time it takes to unlock and reveal the special characteristics worth noting and celebrating as well as bringing to remembrance the stories that were meaningful involving the person you want to honor. It's also good to add humor to the letters. I think it helps to express a full range of emotions and we enjoy laughing at some of the funny things that are shared and written.

THE "SETTING"

We are also highly intentional about how we set up the environment when we share our letters. Imagine with me for a moment, you've just finished the birthday dinner and now it's time to blow out the candles and eat the cake. At this climactic moment, each member of the family places their letter in front of the one being celebrated, in no particular order.

Let's say, in this scenario, we are celebrating Mom's birthday. Each letter presented is personally written to Mom. One by one, Mom reads the letters out loud so everyone can hear what the other family members had written. As she reads her husband's letter, the children hear their father's words of love and affirmation for their mother, and they get to witness how those words touch her heart. At the same time, these words impact their young hearts in a powerful way. As she reads one of her children's letters, the other siblings can hear what that sibling had to say and they wind up cheering each other on.

I want you to imagine, as a parent, what it's like to read letters every year from your children telling you how much they love you, the reasons why and how grateful they are for all the things you do. Trust me, your eyes will flood with tears as you hear firsthand how you have impacted your children in ways you could not have imagined. Sometimes the things they appreciate most are the simplest things that you may not even quantify. When you hear those words from your child's heart and perspective and what it meant to them, it is priceless.

When it's one of the children's birthday, we go through the same routine. Mom, Dad and the other siblings each write a letter to the one being celebrated. Can you even imagine for a moment how you would feel as you heard words of inspiration, fun and affirmation from your other siblings? Many of us walk around starved of these things. What a gift it would be to know how they feel about you, right?

On Dad's birthday, our children get to hear their mother praise their father and give words of affirmation, love and gratitude for all he does for the family. As he reads his children's letters, he is esteemed and honored to hear his children bless him and hear their hearts as they express their love and appreciation for him. Best of all, he is able to hear why they love him. By the way, fathers also cry when they read these letters. Fathers want to know that all they are doing is actually making a difference.

This has been our family's tradition since 1988 and we have no intention of ever stopping. We have never missed a birthday. In fact, years ago, we added Mother's Day and Father's Day to the mix. How great is that! Mom and Dad get two letters a year.

We've been doing this for so long now that when it is letter-reading time, we all start banging our hands on the table shouting "LETTERS, LETTERS, LETTERS!" There is so much excitement and anticipation when we gather for every birthday. Everyone enjoys reading their letters and the others can't wait to hear what everyone else wrote.

It is very interesting and exciting to see things from all different perspectives and gain powerful insights through the lens of each family member and their words. Things you may or may not have seen on your own is brought to your attention through the experiences of each individual. This is especially meaningful when the past year contained particularly difficult times. Noting how they handled trials they've walked through builds confidence that they can do it again when facing the next challenge. As our children have grown older, they have also incorporated childhood memories and stories in the letters which adds a fun journey down memory lane.

BE CREATIVE

As we have carried on this ritual through the decades, most letters have been read at the dining room table. However, as life progressed and our children grew, the experience has had to evolve and cause us to draw on our creativity. If we were on vacation when a birthday occurred, we would adapt the ritual to fit the situation.

For example, on our son Jonathan's birthday a few years ago, we were in Colorado. We decided we would pack our lunches and letters and hike up a mountain trail to a waterfall and sit by the water as he read his letters. One year on my birthday, we drove to the beach for the day. I read my letters there. All of the meaning and importance of the celebration and letter-reading were still there even though we were away from home.

There were challenges as our children got older and moved away, but this tradition is so ingrained within our family that we make sure the letters are done as we gather to read them all together, even if the actual birthday has passed. We find a weekend when everyone can gather and we do it!

There was one change that happened recently that made things very different for us and our letter ritual. Our son, Vinnie, moved to Washington, DC to be part of a church plant. This new season for him was powerful and exciting on so many levels.

Living in another state, we realized that for the first time he would not be home for his birthday. We thought it would be sad that he was going to miss out on being with family and our tradition of reading of the letters. We had not been to DC to visit him yet, so Michael and I thought Vincent's birthday would be the perfect excuse for a trip.

The family letters were written and e-mailed to him by his siblings while Michael and I personally brought our letters with us. I guess we are old school, and prefer the hard copies. On Vinnie's birthday, we found a great place outside to sit down by the wharf and create the moment. We were able to bring the tradition with us, and a touch of home, which Vinnie said meant the world to him.

There is so much flexibility and opportunity as you endeavor to adopt the process of writing letters. Use this time to get as creative as you want, but don't let it spill over into pressure. The bottom line is *just start writing*.

THE OPTIONS TECHNOLOGY GIVES

I understand as I write this book that not everyone has family living nearby. You may be spread out over other states or even countries. In a time where technology is so readily available, there are so many ways to connect despite the distance. There are so many platforms for video chat like Skype, Face Time or Google Hangouts which allow you to see the other person in real time. Some of them even have group video chat capabilities.

Remember, it's the person receiving the letters that actually reads them out loud, so video chat is a solution that works well. If you wanted to, you could send the letters ahead of time via mail or e-mail and then set up a time to video chat so you can all participate and share in the celebratory reading of the letters. Don't let geographical distance create a barrier. Take full advantage of technology.

VIDEO CHAT BIRTHDAY CELEBRATION.

RELIVING LETTERS FROM THE PAST

When our children were young, we would video our letter reading time. Years later, when we watch the videos, the emotions are off the charts. Our children, who are now adults, enjoy hearing themselves with their young voices reading their letters out loud. Capturing the tears, hugs and laughter is beyond priceless. The recording of these moments may prove to become healing tools in the future as one looks back on them in times of reflection, sadness or difficulty.

As we have moved into the grandparent season of our lives, it has caused me to want to record these letter-reading sessions again. It is fantastic to have our grandchildren join in the letter legacy. The joy of giving and receiving more letters with our grandchildren is a treasure. Every grandchild added to the fold is another life we get to celebrate. My husband and I value these letters so much that we don't really want any other gifts. We just want our letters. They are the best gift of all.

A WOVEN TAPESTRY

These letters have become woven into the tapestry of our family legacy. They have become a tradition that will stand the test of time. These letters have been a critical component in framing the culture of our family. You may be asking how all of that was accomplished. All I can say is that first, we just started writing. We remained true to the integrity of the reason for the letters, and we were determined to be consistent each year for every birthday.

To be honest, there were times we were so busy, we would think to ourselves, "Do I even have time to write this letter?"

Deep in our hearts, we knew the effort would speak volumes. Our words would leave an imprint on our loved one's heart that would last forever and sometimes even be life changing.

I can say all of this from a place of experience because we have seen these things happen many times. What we began years ago now translates into: we share how we feel, what we love, and how we are inspired by each other. Over time, it has created a closely woven fabric for our family bringing us together in both beautiful and powerful ways.

It's a living tapestry that will remain
for generations to come.

Through these letters, we have developed our relationships with each other and have established trust and peace within our family. There is a bond that is created through the power of life-giving words that come in the form of a letter that fills each person with confidence, affirmation, praise and love.

We don't have to wonder how our family feels about us or what they think. We *know* their hearts towards us because each of us has reflected, taken the time to write it down and give each other a gift that just keeps giving, the sacred *family letter.*

This vehicle has opened our hearts and has enabled us to share our thoughts and emotions. We all have grown because of it. We have all been changed as a result of entering into this venture together as a family. My heart encourages you to believe this is possible for you, too. Make the decision to begin with the next birthday that is coming up in your family and let your own family tapestry begin!

chapter four

READY, SET, GO!

I'd like to begin this chapter by making a statement, one that I hope will dispel any type of mindset you may have regarding starting this process. I declare, with all the passion within me, that it is never too early nor is it ever too late to begin writing letters to your family, friends or significant people in your life. The only moment that would prove that it is too late is the sorrowful moment of your loved one's very last breath. Don't wait. Don't put it off any longer. Choose to start today!

My intent for this book is simple. Through sharing with you what we have done in our family, you will feel equipped to implement this in yours. I know this may be new for you so let me encourage you to simply keep your heart and mind open. Breathe in, embrace the concept and choose to begin.

> Trust me, the words you need
> to share are inside of you.

HOW TO BEGIN

We began the *family letter* when our son Jonathan was seven and our daughter Jaime was five. They were young and learning how to write in school. We thought since they had to write short stories, why not help them take it to a more personal level and write the family letter. Personal, and with purpose.

When the children were little, our letters were super simple. We wanted them to write and didn't want to make it difficult for them. We wanted it to be fun while they learned the skill of encouragement. As they grew older, we increased the ideas and prompts for the writing and it helped them go to a deeper level of expression. Here is the simplified version we used when our children were younger and beginning the process.

- Tell the person what good you see in them.

- Encourage and praise them in their talents or gifts.

- Tell them why you love them.

For some kids, this might come easily. They can talk about how well their sister plays soccer, or how great their brother is at baseball. School and friends are easy subjects. Usually for their mom, when they are young, they can thank Mom for cooking, helping with homework, and just loving them. For their dad, it is usually thanking him for working so hard for the family, playing with them and having fun together.

CELEBRATE THEIR EFFORTS

These are just easy things that kids can write about and share why they are grateful. Remember, this is a growth process of learning how to communicate. At this stage, the letters may be short in length, and that's okay. Your children are learning to open their hearts and find the words to express themselves. It also takes courage on their part, so be their cheerleader and encourage them as they write.

Recognize what they have written and show your gratitude back with love and affirmation. Whatever you do, don't correct anything that they write! Not the spelling, not the punctuation or even the way they share their thoughts on paper. This is coming from their hearts and it needs to be validated, applauded and received with love.

This may sound uneventful, but by writing these family letters, your children learn how to encourage and share their gratitude for their parents and for their siblings. It opens their eyes and their understanding of why this is important. An even more powerful part of this process is when they receive their own letters filled with love and admiration from the other family members. This is a process they will grow in and become better and better at writing and expressing their thoughts and feelings.

OBSERVER TURNED WRITER

When our youngest son, Vinnie, turned five, he wanted to get involved with the family letter. Over his young life, he watched his family write to each other and heard their words as they were read. One day he wanted in and he wanted in right then. Of course, we all said, "YES!"

His very first letter was on my birthday. It was sweet and very simple. All written in the penmanship of a five-year-old still learning his alphabet and how to form each letter.

"Happy birthday, Mom! Hope you get a lot of gifts. Love, Vinnie"

That was it. But he was so proud and so excited to now be officially part of the family letter. He even colored it for me.

So once again, let me share with you that it is never too early and most of all, it is never too late to start this tradition with your family. My children, now grown, have said that writing letters all these years has really helped them in the work place and in their relationships. They have become incredible encouragers and communicators. We had no idea that when we started this that it would have such impact in other areas of their lives. We are grateful and so are our children. I will share more on this later.

On a side note, the family letter is just as it reads. We keep it within our family. This is something we treasure and value so boyfriends and girlfriends are not participants until they marry into the family. This may come across as harsh, but actually, they really look forward to receiving their "first" letter from all of us. It's like a rite of passage.

Our son-in-law Caleb waited almost five years before he got his first letter and now he is writing letters with us and for us as we write for him. It has been such a fun addition to our time together. Watching Caleb jump in and hone his skills at writing and expressing his feelings towards all of us has been a heartwarming and touching process for everyone. It's sweet to watch his young children listen to him as he reads his letters at our dining room table.

Here is Caleb's first letter to me:

Happy Birthday to my new Mom,

I don't think I could ever give enough thanks for all that you have done for Jaime and I. Both you and Mr. Ronca provided Jaime and I an amazing wedding where your passion to serve and entertain family and friends definitely shined through. Speaking of serving, you sure do know how to whip up a wonderful meal and keep all of our bellies full and happy. What excites me now is watching Jaime's cooking skills grow. I know she is having a blast creating delicious meals and she loves to call you for advice. I knew Jaime would have a gift of cooking when she comes from a Mother like you and Grandma Ronca.

I am also very grateful that God provided Jaime a wonderful Mother, and for Mr. Ronca, a loving wife. As Jaime and I begin this new chapter, I know she will be coming to you for all kinds of advice for motherhood, marriage, cooking, designing, etc. and I can't think of anyone who could fit that role better than you.

Happy Birthday again and I hope you don't mind receiving another birthday letter from your first and only son in law.

Love Always,
Caleb

Together we are raising up the next generation to know and understand the value of life-giving words as they listen with their young hearts to the encouragement and love shared by family members, one to another. The day is coming when my grandchildren will move out of the world of observer to the realm of the writer, too.

chapter five

THE IMPACT

The understanding of why it is important to just begin, regardless of time or dynamics within your family has now been established. It's important to understand why. The convictions of my heart declare this very thought. Everyone, and I mean everyone, even the person whom you may feel has the hardest of hearts, needs to know and to hear how and why someone loves them.

Filling someone's emotional tank with empowering words is not only a fundamental need, but I would dare to say it is critical for the well-being of an individual. These words of life that bring encouragement and affirmation to someone who has never received such a gift can be the integral missing ingredient their soul needs most. This could be the very thing they long for.

They may not even understand what they are missing until they are the recipient of a letter from you sharing how special they are and what their relationship has meant to you. Your words have the power to bring answers to the doubts they have wrestled with over the years. Your words can inspire confidence and build the value they need and have longed to hear. Life is tough, and our words bring life. Speak life, and you will change a life. One of the best ways you can speak life is through the vehicle of a letter.

WHO NEEDS YOUR LETTER

I believe that right now, even as you are reading this chapter, you are thinking of at least one, if not several people that you know who would be greatly impacted by a letter from you. Some thoughts on who these people might be are:

- A mentor who imparted so much into your life.

- A friend who walked through fire with you when you couldn't take another step.

- An estranged relative that you lost contact with because of a disagreement.

- A teacher who made all the difference in your life.

- A parent or parents who need to know how much you appreciated them.

- A grandparent that guided you when you were in times of need.

THE SPOKEN BLESSING

Years ago, when I heard a teaching on the spoken blessing, I decided to travel home to visit my parents with the thought of doing this for them. I spoke to my brothers ahead of time and shared with them the idea of verbally blessing our parents and thanking them for working so hard and providing for us all these years.

We all gathered in the living room and asked our parents to sit on the couch. There were seven of us there sitting in front of our parents, and I could tell our parents were wondering what we were up to. Then, one by one, we began to thank Mom and Dad for working so many jobs to provide, coaching our baseball teams, loving us and so on.

Our parents dropped their heads and covered their faces with their hands and began to weep. I know at this moment, we as siblings were wondering what we had done to make them cry. Our parents lifted up their heads and began to share with us that they were thinking the day before that they were not good parents. When they heard our words, it made them feel so much better and our timely words brought the affirmation they needed so desperately.

I imagine you are wondering if I wrote it all down and yes, I did. They had our words written in a letter which they got to keep and read over and over again whenever they needed the encouragement. Our words brought life and healing. Now think of your parents, and if you are privileged to still have them in your life, write them a letter.

In Proverbs 16:24, NIV it says, *"Gracious words are a honeycomb, sweet to the soul and healing to the bones."* Our words touch and bring healing to someone's heart, spirit, soul and body. The staying power of written words is a gift that remains. They are never forgotten and can be kept in a special place like the treasure they are. On those days when life is challenging, they can pull out that letter, read your words, and get the much-needed encouragement for their soul.

BEYOND THE FAMILY

While this book is primarily about starting a family letter, I believe everyone deserves to receive at least one letter in their lifetime. Take a quiet moment to reflect and allow God to bring to mind those in your path you feel would be blessed by a letter from you. Doing this can be a life-changing moment in your relationship with them. Even more importantly, it could be the tool that brings healing to their heart, spirit and soul.

Remember, words bring life or death, so choose today to be the one who offers life through the power of a letter written specifically for that certain someone who needs a touch from you. Don't underestimate what receiving a letter from you would do to impact another person. Most of us go through life not hearing the words we need to hear and hearing our value and worth come forth from another human being.

> Many live with a question mark looming inside their soul that challenges their self-worth, self-esteem and purpose on this earth.

DON'T HOLD BACK

I've seen so many people at a funeral spill their hearts out with words they wished they had said sooner. Why is it that we wait until a person passes that we then find the words to say how wonderful they were? What is it inside of us that keeps us from giving this very necessary encouragement in life that everyone desires and even craves for at times? Are we afraid we will be rejected? Are we convinced that sharing a few words doesn't really make a difference? Are we thinking, "Well, no one has ever done this for me!" It's time to take the initiative and be the one who steps out first. Your words do bring life and make all the difference in the world.

WORDS THAT CHANGED A LIFE

I remember years ago reading a story that inspired me regarding the power of words. It started out with a young boy walking home from school who dropped his books all over the sidewalk. Looking down, feeling overwhelmed, he just stood and stared at his books. He did not look up in case anyone saw him and made fun of him.

At school, he was the one who was always picked on by the other kids. While he was standing there, feeling dejected, another young man came up, helped him pick up his books and then offered to walk home with him. As they walked, the second young man engaged in conversation and shared a few kind encouraging words with the other boy as they walked home together.

Years later, the young man who dropped his books was the Valedictorian at his class graduation. His topic was on the power of encouragement. As he spoke at the graduation ceremony, he shared about the day he dropped his books. Unknown by anyone at the time, he was on his way home to take his life because he had become so discouraged and felt like a loser.

This gesture and the kind words from the other young man literally saved his life. Words from another human being broke through the darkness that surrounded this young man. The darkness was so heavy that he even despaired of life! Those life-giving words made the difference.

We can't continue to underestimate what words can do. We need to ask the Lord to help us loose our tongue and give us the courage to speak forth encouragement and inspiration to those around us. You never know how you can change a person's life or the way they think of themselves. We all have those days where we experience the condescending thoughts of ourselves or feel so defeated we can't seem to pick ourselves up. What would it mean to receive a phone call from someone who shared some words that encouraged us? What would it mean to our hearts to know that someone sees something special about us or shares their appreciation of our talents or gifts?

Imagine receiving a letter filled with affirmation, recognition and appreciation. It would rock your world because it would be so unexpected. It would give you such a shot of encouragement that you would feel ten feet taller. You would probably feel like you could accomplish anything. It would literally put the wind back in your sails. You would walk more confidently, feel valued and validated by either a family member, friend or loved one.

What are we waiting for? Ask the Lord who needs to receive a letter from you and start the ripple effect of sharing life, love and words that will invade their heart to bring hope and restoration.

Use the space below to write down a few names that come to mind and one or two thoughts of why you need to write them a letter. Is it encouragement, or reconciliation, or affirmation? Write down thoughts like these to inspire you to begin. Once you know your "why", it will help you move forward and write.

WHO   WHY

_____   _____

_____   _____

_____   _____

_____   _____

heart facing you when engaged, and away from you if you are not engaged.

Until you find the man you are going to marry, I want you to wear this ring as a symbol of our commitment to each other as Father and daughter. Wear it as a reminder that I love you unconditionally, and that I will always provide for you and protect you.

The only things I ask of you are that you keep your standards high, love the Lord with your whole heart, stay committed to doing the right thing for the right reason and always strive for excellence.

You are a leader with a special calling on your life. Promise me you will always remember that you are special! You have a tender heart, you are smart, beautiful and athletically awesome. God has truly blessed you!

> *Love,*
> *Daddy*

After she read the letter, he gave her a beautifully wrapped box that held her Claddagh ring. She opened it with great excitement and then her daddy put the ring on her finger. Jaime then grabbed her letter in her hands and ran up and down the hallway in our house shouting "I'm engaged to Daddy!", "I'm engaged to Daddy!" while wildly waving her letter high in the air so all could see. What a moment. I can still see it as if it was yesterday. It is a treasured story to tell for years to come. Well, actually, there's more!

For ten years she wore her daddy's ring, remembering his words and keeping her promise. The time came when Jaime met Caleb, the love of her life, and they married when she was 23 years old. While planning for this glorious day, both Michael and I felt that the segment in the ceremony where the father gives the bride away was just too short, and also a little impersonal. This was a change of covenant from her father to her husband and it needed to be a more memorable moment. What do you think we did?

My husband, dressed in his tux, and Jaime in her Swarovski crystal gown walked down the flower laden aisle towards Caleb. When it came time for the big question, "Who gives this bride away?" my husband answered, "Her mother and father". He then walked Jaime up the steps with her still on his arm and presented her to Caleb.

Everyone must have been thinking, "Where is he going? He needs to let her go so she can walk up alone!" But Michael was intentionally making a moment of it. Once they arrived at the top of the steps, he put Jaime's hand in Caleb's then turned around and stood in front, facing both of them and our guests. He pulled out the letter he had written ten years earlier and shared it out loud with everyone there. He then removed the Claddagh ring from Jaime's hand and gave the ring to Caleb. He then said firmly, but with love, "Caleb, I need you to listen." You can see by the photo that Caleb was a little nervous!

MICHAEL'S "CHARGE" TO CALEB

"Caleb, I have had a covenant with my daughter all of her life where I have loved her unconditionally, protected and provided for her. Today is your wedding day and this is the moment where I am giving to you my precious daughter and entrusting her to you, in a new covenant. I am asking now as her father that you become her protector, her provider, and always love her unconditionally."

There wasn't a dry eye in the house. What a powerful and beautiful memory, and it all started with a letter. A letter written to a thirteen-year-old girl who knew and understood that her daddy loved her, and that one day her daddy would entrust her to another man she would love, her husband.

A MARRIAGE CELEBRATION

When Michael and I celebrated our 38th wedding anniversary, we decided to renew our vows. Since we were going through all the effort of it, we really did it up. We rented a beautiful venue and had a huge celebration. Our children made up our bridal party, and our granddaughter Natalie, who was only 4 months old at the time, was our flower girl and our grandson Kellan, age 5, was our ring bearer. Natalie's dress was made from my original wedding gown as well as the pillow that Kellen carried down the aisle.

Prior to the event, we asked our children if they would be the ones to do the toast for us at the reception. When the moment arrived, we all stood together holding glasses of champagne anticipating what would be shared during the toast. We had no idea, but one by one, our children surprised us and pulled out a letter they each had written to us. They stood in front of a crowd of 150 people and read their words of love and let everyone know how their parent's marriage blessed and impacted their lives.

Our letters had always been a private thing with our family, so this was off the charts to hear our children share their love for us in front of family and friends. Everyone was so deeply touched and shared how they felt they had personally experienced an intimate moment with our family. The tradition of writing letters has also taught our children that special events in life also deserve the recognition of a letter so that the moment is captured and celebrated.

> Writing it down preserves the moment forever in the hearts and minds of your family so they can be cherished for years to come.

OUR CHILDREN READING THEIR LETTERS AT OUR VOW RENEWAL

I would like to share a portion of Jonathan's letter that was read that night at our Vow Renewal:

I want to toast the best parents that I could have ever wished for, Michael and Debi Ronca. Not only have they been incredible parents but they are two of the greatest people you will ever meet. And Yes, I am biased.

Today, we toast to true love. The kind of love that is unconditional, forgiving, patient, deeper than the deepest ocean, and always endures despite the odds. Michael and Debi's love is the kind of love you typically only read about in poetry or see on the big screen. My parents' love reminds me of this quote, "You know you're in love when you can't fall asleep because reality is finally better than your dreams." (Dr. Seuss)

38 years together is an incredible accomplishment. Congratulations!

My parents have taught me many things in life, but perhaps the greatest is unconditional love. I have been blessed to have received it every day for 34 years, even when I pushed buttons just to be sure their love was real, and thank God it was. I believe continually receiving this unconditional love has helped me better understand God's true nature and it has birthed more positive characteristics in my siblings and I than anything else.

Play this game with me. Please raise your hand if when spending time with either of my parents you have ever laughed…been inspired…been helped through a difficult time in your life…been prayed for…learned something helpful or new…been loved unconditionally.

Look around, Mom and Dad. This is your life's ripple effect. These are some of the many important lives you have touched and impacted forever because of your love for God, each other and other people. Like the Beatles famously once said, "and in the end, the love you take is equal to the love you make". May God continue to bless your marriage till the end of time.

Love on Mom and Dad!
Jonathan

chapter seven

LETTER OF FORGIVENESS

When we started the family letter, the first few years we also included letters on Christmas Day. Those were read on Christmas morning before we opened our gifts. Jonathan and Jaime were very young this particular year, and in fact, it was the first Christmas spent in our new home.

During this stage of their childhood, they were very competitive and did not get along. It was the typical brother and sister rivalry and teasing that goes on, but it really bothered Jaime. She felt her brother picked on her and I can attest that he did. We were doing what we could to monitor the situation but more needed to be done.

This particular Christmas, we had the kids read their letters first. Jaime and Jonathan exchanged their letters. This was still a turbulent time with their relationship. As Jaime read her letter from Jonathan, he wrote in his letter that he was sorry for the way he had been treating her, and for being mean and that he was going to try to be a nicer brother. At the same time, as Jonathan read Jaime's letter, she was asking him to stop picking on her and that it made her sad and wanted him to be a nicer brother.

After they read the letters, they looked up at each other, put their arms out and hugged. Forgiveness was issued between them. It was just so unbelievable that their letters to each other brought restoration that probably would have taken longer without them. The letters gave a voice to their struggle which empowered them to fix it! It was powerful. This story is still part of the memory bank we reflect on over the years of what these letters have meant to us and how they have impacted us corporately and individually.

A BROKEN RELATIONSHIP

Are you struggling with a relationship that needs this kind of healing? Sometimes it seems we just can't speak the words in person. A letter can be a safer way to reach out, convey your feelings and seek restoration. You never know how the other person is feeling, or if they miss you, and neither of you may feel you know how to bring back what was lost. Pray, and ask the Lord for the words to share and begin to write.

Be courageous and kind when you reach out to the loved one with whom you have a lost or broken relationship. If God can speak individually to children to share their pain and bring restoration, I believe he can do the same with you. Personally, I have been in a situation where a family member chose to shut the door on our relationship. It was their choice. I, too, am praying about what to write and when to send a letter with the hope of restoration.

We are all in this together. Each of us has struggles and we simply must never give up. It's worth a try to sit down and write your feelings out. Getting that first line written can be a challenge but it's not impossible. Take a moment to go back to chapter three where I lay out the Rules for Engagement. Choose a few of those ideas, pray and ask the Lord to help you write that which will touch the heart of your family member, friend or co-worker. I will tell you that this process isn't just for them. God absolutely uses this process for your good as well.

God knows what this person needs to hear. I know that by His Spirit, He will inspire you to write the very words that will capture their heart and their mind that can begin reconciliation, or maybe even just crack open the door a little bit that had been slammed shut years ago. Make it your prayer that God will allow the conversation to be renewed again between you both. I know this can be so difficult and tender. It will take courage on your part, but it is better to try and to not let any more time go by than later have regrets that you did not reach out. The letter will allow you to share your thoughts while giving you a safe place to pour out your heart.

> Your words can be the key that
> unlocks a broken relationship.

Many families lose their connection, especially after both of the parents are deceased. Parents are often the core reason everyone gets together on holidays and vacations. If the relationship between the siblings is not strong, then little by little, the family drifts apart. Sometimes it is because of a disagreement, but other times, it's because we get busy and are not intentional about staying connected with each other.

While my mother was dying from pancreatic cancer, she shared with me that she was so afraid our family would fall apart after she was gone. We had some difficult times together after she passed, but little by little, we have nearly all reconnected. Throughout all of my life, I have never written any of my brothers a letter. I've only done this with my children. I've expressed myself in person to them, but I know that if I were to take the time, pray and ask the Lord what to say to each one of them in the form of a letter, they would be so shocked, but also it would be so impactful.

We have not communicated like this over the years, so receiving a letter that tells them why I love them, what things I admire about them or even sharing some memories of growing up together could be just the thing we need to re-establish a stronger bond with each other. So, what's my next project? I will write letters to my siblings and then look forward with hope and expectation that my words will bring us closer and bridge any gaps that have existed over the years.

If this is something you want to tiptoe into, I would love for you to join me online. I have a private Facebook group called "The Family Letter", where you can ask for feedback about the letters you have written if you feel it will help you. You can also share ideas and insights. It is a safe space where you can even practice if you need it. Let's share this journey together and inspire one another with our breakthrough stories. It's empowering!

chapter eight

LETTERS TO THE
NEXT GENERATION

The concept of a generation is something to ponder. Specifically, it is a measured segment of time between the parents and their offspring. There is a significant gap in the ages between them, and for that reason, older generations have so much more to share and impart to the younger generations. Titus 2 encourages both the "older men and women" to teach the younger. During biblical times, it was a custom or tradition for the older generation to share the stories of what the Lord had done and the mighty works He performed.

Psalm 145:4-7 NIV says, "One generation commends Your works to another, they tell of Your mighty acts. They speak of the glorious splendor of Your majesty and I will meditate on Your wonderful works. They tell of the power of Your awesome works, and I will proclaim Your great deeds. They celebrate Your abundant goodness and joyfully sing of Your righteousness."

This powerful blessing of the Lord from one generation to another comes from sharing the details of what God has done, on who He is, and how His goodness was evident in all He did. As I look at this scripture from a natural perspective, I see an amazing model of how we can follow through and impart this blessing to the next generation of our precious grandchildren.

As the older generation, we need to take the time to share with our grandchildren, the great things they have done, who they are as individuals and also the godly characteristics we see in them. This will prove to be an impartation that will leave a mark on their lives for years to come. Writing a letter to our grandchildren and allowing them to receive from us a "blessing" from our viewpoint is a lifelong treasure. One day, they can even show their children what their grandparents saw in them and what they loved about them. Priceless!

A GRANDPARENT'S PERSPECTIVE

If you are a grandparent, I believe you will agree with me that we have a whole different view point or perspective as we observe the lives of our grandchildren. We have an eye of wisdom and a lifetime of experience that allows us to see what maybe even the parents cannot see. How many stories have you heard over the years about how a grandparent saw something unique in their grandchild? They recognized it and encouraged their grandchild in what they observed.

These observations many times wind up becoming the grandchild's truth and what they believe about themselves and their future legacy. Some have gone on to become famous athletes, preachers and business leaders all because of what their grandparent saw in them. The greatness they saw and shared gave their grandchildren wings to fly. Some grandparents have the opportunity to raise their grandchildren providing the stability and love needed to nurture them. I applaud the grandparents who have done this because it helps establish the strong foundation your grandchildren need to believe in the possibility of a great future for themselves. You are a hero in my eyes!

Grandparents, you have a role to play that is unique and different than the parents. Press in and start being intentional about watching your grandchildren and speaking life over them. I encourage you to gather your thoughts and your personal inspiration for them and leave your words of life written down for their keeping. A great time to start would be on their birthday or another special event happening in their life. There is something so wonderful about being grandparents.

Whether you are a new grandparent or have had the joy of watching your grandchildren grow, get married and now have children of their own, you are crowned with a glorious legacy. Being a grandparent is a special honor and each of us has the potential to make a tremendous impact on our grandchildren's lives.

A GRANDPARENT'S LETTER

While writing this book, my friend Melody told me a precious story about her grandparents and gave me permission to share it with you. Melody is the granddaughter of evangelists Charles and Frances Hunter, a couple who loved the Lord deeply, and had one of the most outstanding healing ministries in the world. Their intimacy with the Lord enabled them to hear His voice in ways that brought the miraculous down from heaven to earth bringing healing to the masses.

If any of you had the blessing of being in any of their services, then you know what I am talking about. If you did not get to meet them, please contact Joan Hunter Ministries and you can see the generational blessings and legacy of these amazing grandparents that still live on through their daughter Joan and down in to the lives of their grandchildren and great grandchildren.

In Charles and Frances' latter years, age began to take its toll on their physical bodies. It was becoming more and more of a reality that they might pass away before Melody got married. Melody's grandmother was not doing well and had been in and out of the emergency room with various complications. One day, after Frances was out of the hospital and had miraculously returned to their ministry offices, Melody visited her.

As they met, Melody said, "Grandma, I want to ask you something but I don't want it to hurt you or make you sad." Frances responded with a nod and a smile. Melody said, "I am worried because I don't know if you will get to meet the man I am going to marry. I'm sad and it makes me upset at the possibility that you may be gone by the time I get married. I want him to have something special from you and from Poppa. Will you write him a letter? Will you write him something that would let him know how much you would love him and would have wanted to know him? Will you tell him how special you and Poppa are and how much you love each other?"

At the time, Melody was in her early twenties, and there was not a significant man in her life. She was believing God for the man He had in mind for her. Her sisters were married and each of their husbands got to meet Charles and Frances. Frances told Melody that she would write the letter, sign it and seal it.

Here are some amazing details about this letter: Frances dictated the letter for her secretary to type. The letter was signed by Charles and Frances, placed in a pink envelope (their favorite color) then sealed. The envelope is addressed: To the Husband of Melody. Frances gave the sealed envelope to Melody and this is my favorite part: this letter is being protected in a safety deposit box.

Frances passed away the following year and her secretary passed away about two years later. Eleven months after Frances passed way, Charles went to be with her in heaven. Frances did not let Melody read the letter or hear the dictation—this means that NO ONE knows what the letter says.

Even though the letter is locked away, Melody has plans for it. Once she is engaged and the wedding date is announced, the letter will be read out loud for the first time at the actual rehearsal dinner. Can you imagine?! My heart is excitingly thinking of all of the possible things they could have written, and the anticipation of what everyone will hear when the seal of this precious letter is opened for the very first time and read for all to hear.

I can imagine a respectful silence, a sacred reverence that will fill the room as this letter is revealed. No dry eyes. In fact, tears will flow in abundance. A mother will hear her parents' blessing to her daughter. A granddaughter will hear her grandparents' blessing to her husband. All will be so deeply touched to hear their heart and prayers for this special man and their marriage. There are really no words to describe the beauty, strength and power of this moment for Melody and her husband. It is so special on every level. Words of life from one generation to the next, sharing and leaving a legacy that will stand the test of time.

Thank you, Melody, for sharing this priceless idea with us. One day soon, you will hear what is in that letter. Knowing how spirit-led your grandparents were and how they heard the Lord so clearly while they walked this earth, you can know that their words will be spot on. No doubt there will be a little surprise here and there but truly a profound blessing straight from the heart of God for you and your husband for your wedding day. Although they never got to meet him in the natural, their spiritual eyes have seen and their ears have heard what the Lord Himself loves about your future husband, and you my friend, have it all written down in a letter by their own hand and heart to treasure forever.

So, grandparents, can you hear the call? It is time to step into the arena and begin to write letters to your grandchildren that will impact them for years to come. Remember, it's never too late to start. I so wish I had my grandparent's thoughts towards me written down. It would be amazing to be able to read them, and after all these years, I know their words would conjure up memories that may have been forgotten by now.

It would be so inspiring to be able to share with my children, their great-grandparents' feelings about me and also give them a glimpse as to how their great-grandparents thought years ago. But alas, I don't have this gift. So, I have decided that I am going to be intentional with my grandchildren and leave them a blessing and a legacy from Nana! Of course, Papi will be writing his own letters, and our grandchildren will be doubly blessed. In fact, I may borrow my friend's idea and write a letter to my grandchildren that will be read to them on their wedding day.

Oh, there are so many reasons to begin writing letters. What joy!

chapter nine

THE PERSPECTIVE

I wanted to dedicate this chapter to highlighting what these letters have meant to our children over the years and how they feel about them now, since all have become adults. They were each asked to share their thoughts, so this chapter is all about them and from their perspective.

From Jonathan:

> *We are blessed to have a very loving and close-knit family. I truly believe it's because of our faith in God and these letters that have kept us bonded over the years. It's always the best feeling in the world to read these letters on my birthday and actually hear all the beautiful and*

encouraging things my loved ones have to say about me. It fills me up with so much love and joy!

I remember this process teaching me at a young age to get more deeply in touch with my feelings and how to have confidence to share those feelings with others. When I was younger, my sister and I unfortunately fought a lot, but these letters were such a beautiful way for me to express how much I loved her and vice versa, despite our usual sibling rivalry. They always healed any wounds in the heart and reminded me both how much I am loved and how much I love my family members.

So many families don't have an outlet to express these emotions on a consistent basis much less in a deep and meaningful way. Unfortunately, over time, family members can build up a lot of bitterness and resentment towards each other. If not properly expressed and processed, before you know it, relationships become strained or even worse, severed.

Writing these letters to my family continuously opens my heart and allows for healing, love and connection multiple times throughout every year. At every birthday we are inspired and moved as both the writer, the receiver and even the listener while the letters are being read aloud around the dinner table. We like to add humor in there to keep them fun as well.

Most people don't feel they are loved or accepted by their parents and/or siblings and that makes me terribly sad. I can tell you that because of these letters, I know and have proof that I am fully loved and supported by my entire family. That is one of the most priceless gifts one can receive.

Commit to adding this sacred and loving tradition to your family for at least one year and see if it wasn't one of the best decisions you've ever made for you and your family.

Thank you, Jonathan. Well, I guess you can tell he is our firstborn. Jonathan, you have always loved sharing details about everything in life. What you conveyed has truly captured the essence of our family letters. You have a special tenderness and compassion. You live life with passion and you have a beautiful spirit. These qualities have always showed up in your letters, and we have all been blessed by your words.

Jonathan, you are loved!

From Jaime:

These letters have been a great tool that my parents initiated to bring our family closer together, especially as siblings. It is so easy to go day after day and year after year without telling your sibling that you love them, you are proud of them, or the qualities they have that you admire.

The letters we have done over the years are a way to be intentional about communicating these things. Without them, I don't believe I would be as close to my brothers or parents as I am today. It's a tradition I have been greatly impacted by while I was growing up and even now into my adult years.

I plan on continuing this tradition with my own kids since I've seen and experienced the benefit first hand. When my son, Kellan, turned 6 we wrote our first letter to him. He has sat around my parents table watching and listening to us read letters to each other and now we feel he is old enough to start receiving his own letters. Our daughter Natalie isn't quite old enough as of the time I am writing this, but her day is coming. By then, Kellan will be ready to start writing a letter to her as her big brother on her birthday.

I can hardly wait to watch the next generation carry on the tradition of our family letter. I will be the Mom hearing my children share their feelings of love towards me. I will be experiencing what my own mother has felt as we, her children, have written our letters to her. Okay, heart…get ready!

Thank you, Jaime. I know you are imparting the gift of love and encouragement to your children and you too will reap the joy of hearing their hearts toward you as they begin to write their own letters. You are so right when you talk about getting your heart ready, because you are an incredible mom and your children know and feel your love and will have many beautiful things to write to you. Your letters will become your treasures. Your compassion, kindness and steadfastness are evident in all that you do, and you are raising a family that is strong and full of life. I am so happy you are passing this sacred tradition on to the next generation.

Jaime, you are loved!

From Vinnie:

> *Mom, thanks for asking us to share about what the letters have meant to us. I think the letters have helped grow me in a variety of ways over the years. Practically speaking, I think they have made me a better writer and helped me to be able to express thoughts and emotions by putting them into words.*
>
> *I remember my first few letters were only one sentence long. For example, "I hope you get a lot of gifts!" I've definitely come a long way since then and would like to thank you, Mom and Dad, for encouraging me along the way as I learned to write and share.*
>
> *The letters have also helped me grow in my ability and willingness to be vulnerable, share my emotions with someone, and encourage them with loving words. Those are skills that have definitely become useful as I've navigated different situations in life.*

Finally, being on the receiving end of the letters has gone a long way towards my having confidence in who I am and that I am loved. Reading the encouraging and loving words of those that are closest to you out loud is a powerful thing. It reinforces those qualities that others see in you that you may doubt or forget about.

You and Dad always do a great job of vocalizing that we are loved and cherished, but it is also so helpful to have those words on paper so I can look back on them and be encouraged.

The letters certainly grew us closer together as a family and encouraged us to be more open with our feelings towards each other. Thank you so much Mom and Dad for starting that tradition!

Thank you, Vinnie! I know you have shared with us that when you were in the role of a sport's writer, you felt that all the writing you did over the years played a part in helping your write those articles. Knowing that the letters have also helped you grow in the ability to be vulnerable and open with your feelings truly blesses me. This, my son, also prepares you to be an awesome husband one day! Your future wife will be blessed. A man who can share his heart is powerful! Your sensitivity, sense of humor and your heartbeat for truth are a strong foundation for your life.

Vinnie, you are loved!

Now, earlier I spoke about the letters being for the family only, and that boyfriends or girlfriends did not receive a letter until they married into the family. It meant that much to us. So, now you will get to hear from our "other" son, Caleb, Jaime's husband.

From Caleb:

When Jaime and I started dating and I was invited to the birthday dinners, I always enjoyed listening to everyone's letter. I believe the letters were one of the stepping stones of being part of the family. Reading them reminded me that we are all connected and how involved we are in each other's lives. The letters were like a re-cap of the last year with words of love and encouragement for dreams or goals for the future.

It's amazing how all the letters carry a similar theme for each individual for that birthday year. My mom writes handwritten letters to us pretty frequently, most are short letters but they are always of encouragement and love. I think most people don't write letters anymore and it's a lost sign of love.

The birthday letters are intimate. It takes time to remove ourselves from everyday life in order to reflect on the person we are writing about. Sometimes, it's hard to get started on paper but once we open our heart it becomes pretty fluid and natural to write about the people we love.

Jaime and I wrote a little letter to Kellan for his 6th birthday and I remember how much joy it brought him to hear kind and encouraging words. This is a tradition that we will continue with our family.

Thank you, Caleb. I know we were all so excited when we wrote you your very first letter after you and Jaime got married. It truly is a stepping stone of being part of the family. It was fun and everyone willingly rose to the occasion. It is equally exciting to see you now engaged in writing letters to each of us and now for your own children. You are an amazing blessing and son to us Caleb, and you are an incredible husband and father, too. Your love is deep and constant with your family.

Caleb, you are loved!

Our children were excited and honored to share their thoughts with you regarding our family letter practice. I hope their words encouraged you even more to begin this tradition. Going through our collection of letters over the years, I opened up the family vault and pulled out a few for you to read so you can get an idea of what we did. You will find letters from when our children were young, and then some from later years. There are a few in this chapter and another collection at the end of the book. Reading the letters from when our children were very young will really demonstrate that at times, the letters truly are very simple. The important thing was that they took the time to write. As the children grew older, the letters became longer and the content took on a deeper level of emotion and encouragement.

I would like to point out that these letters have never been read by anyone else but us. I wasn't sure about making our personal stories public, but my family was insistent I include them to give examples and insight to our tradition. This is your personal invitation to join us at our table and share in our family letters. Welcome to our world.

Our letters are honest, loving and funny. They have progressed over the years in content. One recent Mother's Day, my son Jonathan's letter was written in the form of a rap. In fact, he had to read it to me so we could have the "right beat." It was so much fun. The more we do these letters, the more creative we get. It really adds to the whole experience for the family. I've also included the first letter from our grandson Kellan. He was only four at the time, so he told my daughter what he wanted to say. So, she wrote it and he signed it. He is learning and it's precious to observe.

Dear Papi,

Happy Birthday Papi!!!

This was the BEST Christmas EVER!

I love you because you're funny & because you give me cool presents. And I like to swim in your pool, and sometimes you come to my house.

I hope you have a great birthday!

Kellan

Dear Dad,

Happy B-Day! You've been a great dad all these years. I'm proud to call you my dad. You're a great supporter to all of us. You always support us when we make a decision. Another thing about you is you let us make our own choices. As long as they're not anything dangerous or something. But the thing I like about you the most is you don't care about materials on your B-Day. I remember that you said your favorite part of your B-Day is the letters. I hope you have a wonderful B-Day and enjoy the letters.

Love,
Vincent (8 years old)

Dear Mom,

*I thought you were 29 years old...but you were 39???
I am confused...anyway...happy birthday...you are the
best mom in the world! I hope you get lots of presents and
have fun. Boy, you are old now, in fact you are almost as
old as dad. But you look marvelous!*

*Love,
Vincent (7 years old)*

Dear Dad,

*I love you so much! Happy Belated B-Day! Sorry these
letters are late, but don't worry we still love you. Well, I
hope you know how much you mean to me. I don't know
how I would have gotten through all my problems w/
out you in my life. You're such a wise, wise man. And I
really appreciate all that you do for me. I know you do
so much for me behind the scenes and you think I don't
know. But I do and I'm really grateful. And I'm really
proud of you for jumping into this new job and working
2 jobs. It shows how brave you are. Well, I love you with
all my heart and don't worry, no matter how old I get I'll
always be Daddy's little girl!*

PS – I'm quitting soccer!!!!!

*Love,
Jaime (14 years old)*

Happy Birthday to the Most Beautiful Woman on Earth!!!

Here's to celebrating 61 years of an amazing person. I must say, you never cease to amaze me. You are a genuinely kind, loving person who has a heart the size of Texas. You are smart and courageous and always thinking of how you can bless others. You are beautiful inside and out and you are a STRONG WOMAN OF GOD, and like I always say, you have a direct line to God.

But now, you have reminded people, and shown some for the first time, your talent and abilities in theater production. It's amazing how you have not written a play in years, yet it came so naturally and easy to you. And you pulled it off beautifully, even with a cast and stage crew who had never helped with a play before. All the feedback you received from people is a testament to your work and how God works through you, always. You have such a gift, that's indescribable.

I feel so blessed to be able to say you're MY Mom. I, selfishly would like to keep you all to myself, but I know you have so many blessings to bestow among others and the world, so I must share you. And Kellan is the luckiest kid to have such an awesome Nana. He loves you so much.

Thank you for all your love and encouragement over the 30 years I've been on this earth. Thank you for being a role model as to what a Godly woman should look like and how to be selfless. It's an understatement to say you have helped many people, whether its spiritually, financially or physically. I know God is not done using you for his purpose, as you embark on a journey with a new ministry. I pray God's hand is upon you. Once again, you never cease to amaze me.

And to close with words from one of my friends: "I seriously picture your mom waking up perfectly made up with perfect hair and walking around in a long satin robe". (And I picture you Mom with your hair blowing in the wind, even when you're inside)! I love you more than you know!!

> *Love,*
> *Jaime, your favorite*
> *daughter of all time.*
> *(30 years old)*

Dear Dad,

Thank you for always being there for us! You are the BEST Dad in the world!! You always have time for us no matter how busy you are. You wrestle, watch tv, play games, go swimming with us, and go to our sporting events; which is an accomplishment all by itself! Thank you so much Dad for always working hard to support the family. You would work all day just to supply our family with food and clothes.

You always give a 150% and that and other fine businessman qualities like honesty, love appreciation, diligence, perseverance, and brains are really setting a good example for Jaime, Vinnie and I. Without you, our family would not survive under any conditions. Another great quality about you is that you always put the family first. You would rather spend your money to support the family than treating yourself to something. You are the most UNSELFISH man I know (and that's a fact)! We all love you and appreciate all you have done for us! Happy Father's Day Dad!

> *Love,*
> *Jonathan*
> *(13 years old)*

Dear Daddy,

You are a good Daddy, because you wrestle with me, you watch real movies with me sometimes.

> *Love,*
> *Vincent*
> *(4 years old - spoken by*
> *Vinnie, written by Mom)*

Dear Dad,

HAPPY FATHER'S DAY! If there is one Dad out there that deserves a full day of recognition, it's you. I can't begin to express how great of a father you have been to Jaime, Jonathan (Johnny) and I. But since this would be a very short letter otherwise, I'll give it a shot and see if I can put it into words for you.

Now that I'm an adult and have become a victim of corporate America's constant draining of my time and energy, I can truly appreciate all you did for us growing up. You have always done a great job of making time for us despite your hectic schedule. I know when I get home from work every day, I am exhausted and just want to plop on the couch (which I usually do). Knowing this now, I realize how much of a sacrifice it was for you when you would come home and wrestle with me every night after work. It seems like a small act, but I remember having so much fun playing with you and I'm so glad you made the effort to spend some quality time with me.

Not only that, but I'm sure you spent countless hours helping me with my math homework. Sorry to report, but your efforts may have been somewhat fruitless in that area. Nonetheless, it was appreciated and it surely helped down the road. One of my favorite things about you though, is that I know I can come to you with any of my problems and get great advice. It can be something trivial or life-changing, but either way I know I can trust the advice you give me and will benefit from it. I know I am a better man today because of your experiences you've shared with me and life lessons you've taught.

Just know that I will always be coming to you when I come across something in life that I'm unsure about and that I take your words to heart. Above all, Dad, I want to thank you for providing me with a living example of the kind of man I want to grow up to be. In business, spiritually, and as a (future) husband, I can model myself after you and know I'll be a success. You have done a great job of instilling the Word of God in each of us growing up and have made our household a Godly one. I can look at you and see how you treat your family, employees and friends and see what it means to be a man of God. Thank you for all you've done to teach us, grow us and love us. You're the best Dad in the infinite Universe! I love you so much!

Love,
Vinnie (22 years old)

Dear Mom,

I hope you realize how special you are to me. You're a great mother in everything you do. And I'm really proud of you for everything you do around the house. I mean, I wouldn't have grown up to be such a perfect child if I didn't have such perfect parents, right? You're an awesome person inside and out. You've got a good heart and are always thinking of others. That's a great quality. I don't know how I would survive without you. Especially in a house full of guys. So, as you can see you mean a lot to me. You're beautiful, and still look young, even though the digits are getting a little high. (j/k). And I appreciate how you're always there for me. I can always count on you, no matter what it is. Just want to say thanks. Happy Mother's Day!

PS. Can I get my belly button pierced????????

> *Love,*
> *Jaime*
> *(12 years old)*

If you would like to read some of the letters the children wrote to each other, I have put a collection of them and others in the Keepsake File at the end of the book. It may help to inspire your children on how to write to their siblings. I've also included letters between Michael and myself, and one written to Caleb as he celebrates his first Father's Day. The "rap" letter to me is also there so you can see the freedom in which letters were written and the creativity that can be tapped into each time you write. There are no limitations to what you can do.

chapter ten

THE LAST LETTER AND MORE

I want to share with you some other ideas of great times to give someone a special event letter. Birthdays, Mother's Day and Father's Day have been our constant tradition, but there have been other life events when we felt a letter would be welcomed and appreciated.

The harsh reality is we are not promised tomorrow. With that in mind, I have intentionally written notes and letters my children would find in case something was to ever happen to me or my husband. I've heard many people wishing they could have spoken with a loved one before they passed away. Finding notes and letters can offer comfort and healing to those left behind. It's not about always focusing on something potentially tragic happening, rather it is about intentionally having a message prepared filled with words of life and love that your loved ones will value dearly in the months and years to come.

Being up close and personal, I want to share with you one of the most tender moments that I have experienced in our family. Filled with emotion that covers the spectrum from deep pain to eventual comfort and peace, I share with you a beautiful example of the last letter.

THE LAST LETTER

When my father was ill with cancer and admitted to the hospital for his final days, we happened to be home in Philadelphia for a visit. We knew my dad's time was short and my children had commitments back in Houston and could not stay. Together, they all said, "We want to write Grandpop a letter." As their only grandfather, he was very special to them. They went back to their grandparent's house, and each wrote him a letter.

They went down memory lane and thanked their grandfather for all of the times at the beach, riding the waves together, learning how to play Skip Bo with him, doing puzzles, and so much more. During this time, he was in and out of consciousness, so they didn't have time to personally read the letter to him. We decided to give them to Grandma, and she would read the letters to him when he was awake.

I was able to be there for this heartbreaking and incredibly tender moment as my mother read each letter to my father. I can still see the tears. I can still see the love and resignation as my father was reminded he was an awesome grandpop. He left this world knowing he made an impact on my children that will never be erased from their hearts. He also left this world knowing he was loved more deeply than he ever realized because of what was written in those last letters of love.

Dear Grandpa,

I know you're not feeling very well with the pneumonia and cancer but I just wanted to let you know how much I love and appreciate you. From when I was a little kid I remember that you would always play with me. Whether it was Skip-Bo, hitting golf balls in the backyard, dominoes or anything else you always made it a blast. I remember you would even go ride the waves with us down at Ocean City.

Not many grandpas surf with their grandchildren. But that's what makes you special. You go above and beyond your duties as a grandfather. I just wish we could have come up to see you more often. Oh, and by the way I want to thank you again for keeping your full head of hair so I won't go bald.

Anyway Grandpa, it's been hard for me to see you in the hospital like this. I have always thought of you as a strong man and seeing you in the hospital hurts. But considering you made it this long proves how strong you are. I found out that you were possibly going to die and it scared me. But when I found out that you gave your heart to the Lord, I was really comforted.

Although I may not see you again alive I will always know that I'll see you up in heaven. There we will both have heavenly bodies and who knows, maybe we will go ride some waves together. I love you so much Grandpa and I'll see you in heaven.

Love,
Vincent

In his final moments, life and love between generations were shared and embraced.

In continuing with this thought, I know that one day I will sit down and write my last letter to my family and put it in a safe place for them to collect after my passing. This will be my last thoughts of love for each of them. Because my family knows me so well, I know they will be looking for a letter because it has become such a part of who we are as a family.

I want to gently encourage anyone reading this book that might know your time is short to please take a moment to write your letter of love to your family. They will be comforted by your words and feel you close in their hearts. Ask God, and He will lead you in what to write.

Travel - Whenever my husband and I travel, I write each child a hand-written note with all of the things I love about them and how special they are to me. If something were to ever happen to us on our travels, our children would have these letters as messages of love whispered to them while they grieve.

Senior Prom - I would slip a hand-written note under their bedroom door while they were getting dressed on prom night, telling them how proud I was of them and all the things we were able to celebrate together in their senior year. This letter recognized that one season in their life was ending and the next was about to begin. I've done this for both of my sons and my daughter. Don't think that your sons will not enjoy getting this note! It creates a moment where you both pause and reflect how time has flown by and how they are now growing into their next phase of life.

College – For college, I take this process to another level. When each child graduates from high school, I create a video for them. I start with writing a letter telling the story of their life from birth to high school graduation, highlighting special moments along the way. I take their photo from birth and incorporate photos throughout their growing up years and chronicle birthdays, holidays, vacations, and other fun times that are personal to each child.

The final photo is their high school graduation picture. I collect all of their photos and include them in a video slideshow. You can have professionals do this or find a simple computer application to help you do it yourself. I then record myself reading the letter to go along with the photos on the video.

After the car is packed full of our child's college gear, we as a family sit down and the video is played. Everyone sees it for the first time together. It's a beautiful way to send off your son or daughter as they embark on this new journey.

They love seeing their childhood on video, plus it's a powerful visual tool to remember wonderful times together and to acknowledge how much they have grown along the way. After lots of tears and hugs, we get in the car and drive them off to college. I give them one copy to take with them, and of course, we keep one at home as backup.

Graduations – This is always a great time to celebrate and affirm the accomplishments of meaningful educational milestones. These can be more personal and detailed than the typical store-bought graduation card. Grandparents, this is your opportunity as well to celebrate with a personal letter from you. It will mean so much to your grandchildren.

Christmas - Every year when I pack up the Christmas decorations, I grab a piece of paper and write, "Merry Christmas - I love you, Mom", or something simple and sweet like that. Each year, when the boxes are opened up, they find a short note from me at the beginning of the festive season. I also do this with the thought in mind that if the Lord calls me home before the next Christmas, my children will find a note from me when they open those boxes filled with decorations. I know it will touch them and give them a hug from me from heaven. They know how much I love Christmas, and I know this would mean so much to them.

New Parent - As my children have begun having their own children, I write a special letter to bless the new parents. Each addition is a blessing and causes the parents to grow and stretch themselves. A letter of love and belief at the start of this beautiful, tiring and amazing journey is an important encouragement and commemorates this milestone in their lives. At the time I wrote this book, Jaime and Caleb were having their third and last child in a matter of days. I thought about what that meant and decided to write them a letter. I encouraged them to embrace this moment knowing it would be their last experience in the birthing process and to soak it all in and seal it in their hearts and minds.

CONNECT

If we ever sat down to share our thoughts, we could all come up with some incredible ideas for writing letters. If you haven't already, I would love for you to join the conversation in my Facebook group, "The Family Letter", and share your writing ideas.

Let's inspire and help each other go to the next level by communicating our feelings and words of encouragement to our loved ones. I look forward to hearing about your loved ones response when they read your letter. Share the story of how you started this new tradition and initiated a new culture of honor in your home through the letters you write.

Be courageous. Be kind. Empower through encouragement and be the person who makes a difference in other's lives through the power of your written words. Pray and believe there will be a ripple effect from your efforts. Hearts and souls will be made whole through the value of your words.

Remember, it's never too late to start. Today is a new day, so embrace the chance for a new beginning. Ignite the flame within your family and your important relationships. It is truly life changing. I'll be looking for your stories and celebrating your victories through the letters you have written from your heart. Carpe diem!

My Letter to You, my Valued Reader,

I am thrilled you have finished reading this book and am hopeful it has made an impact on your heart. Please feel my deep encouragement toward you to begin your new adventure in writing letters. It truly is a simple thing to do, yet at the same time, it can be one of the most powerful things you will ever do.

Whether you are still raising your family or your children are grown and on their own, this is a tool that will help you change the culture in your home to one of honor. It will help you establish and deepen the love and value you have for one another. It will afford you the opportunity to speak life to your family. Now is the perfect time to start.

If you are blessed to still have your parents with you, by all means, they need to hear how and why you love them. Have no regrets. Tell them now while you can. Secretly in their hearts, perhaps they long to hear from you. If you have lost close relationships over the years, be the one who extends a hand to bridge that gap by thoughtfully writing a letter.

Believe you have the words inside you. Reflect on what that individual meant to you and let the words fall out on paper. Being intentional will bring you to a place where you will become the one who creates change, inspires hope and instills confidence in those who receive your letter.

You may be the one who brings this life-giving process to the next generation. Whatever category you fall in, remember, in the end, it's all about finding the words to convey your feelings, and sharing them so they will touch the heart, soul and spirit of those you love and care about in your life.

Take a moment and step away from the fast pace of society and create something with a personal touch that will produce life and extend to the next generation. You, my friend, are the key to all of it happening. It begins with you. What a powerful thought and opportunity for you. Go for it. I believe in you.

Be courageous and take a step into a realm of speaking life. You will never regret making the choice. I look forward to hearing from you on Facebook. Oh, the stories we will hear and the lives that will be changed by your heart felt, life-giving words.

With warmth & affection,
Debi

KEEPSAKE FILE

The Vin "Man"

Happy 13th BIRTHDAY!!! I can't believe my little brother is no longer a kid. You're growing up too fast for me. Pretty soon you'll be able to beat me up. (but probably not). But you are the cutest and the coolest little brother I could ever have. I can tell you will turn into a great man. Just remember to stay strong in what you believe in. Well, I hope you have an awesome 13th Birthday.

PS: remember: you're not a boy, not yet a man!!

Love,
Jaime
(17 years old)

Dear Jaime,

HAPPY BIRTHDAY! So now when you call yourself 17 you are finally telling the truth! Thanks for always picking me up at school and taking me places I need to go. I love going in your firebird!! Maybe one day that will be my car! Remember, I'm gonna be 12 soon. By the way, I got good grades this year, and I know it was because of your help. Thanks for being patient with me, when I know I am driving you crazy, but what are sisters for anyway. Have a great B-day and enjoy your new system in your car!

Love,
Vincent
(11 years old)

Jonathan,

First and foremost, I have to get one thing off my chest— Gig'em!! Now that that's out of the way, I'll wish you a happy birthday. HAPPY BIRTHDAY!! Glad we are getting to celebrate you in August. But seriously, I really do want to wish you a great birthday, because you deserve it. You are a wonderful brother to me and always have been.

It was awesome having you live here the past two years. It was a good chance to actually interact with you since I wasn't really able to do anything but eat and watch TV when you lived at home before college. I loved always going to play tennis, tips, homerun derby, etc. with you. Oh, and it was great having a workout partner for a while, even though you forced me to do those wide-grip pull-ups which inevitably led to my shoulder injury which shall haunt me for the rest of my life. But other than that, it was great. Haha just kidding!

You taught me so much over the years. From working out, to girls, to life in general. You have been a great influence on me and have filled me with great advice and I truly appreciate it. I know you have always wanted the best for me which came to light again once I was deciding between colleges. Although I didn't make the decision you were hoping for, I appreciate your passion in trying to get me to a good school and it makes me so happy to know that you'll still support me in a rival school. We will see who's victorious come Thanksgiving.

Anyways, I will miss you when you move to Dallas, but I wish you the best with your real estate career. You'll do great. Thank you so much for being my brother and just always being there for me. I love you and happy birthday!

Love,
Vinnie
(17 years old)

Happy 21st Birthday Vinnie!!!!!!!

I always thought it would be weird when you turned 21, just because you're my little brother and the baby of the family. And you know what......it is a little weird. It makes me feel old so I can't imagine how it makes mom and dad feel. But as weird as it is for us, it seems normal in the sense that you are mature and have your head on straight. You're a responsible young man, even though when you do have a job you manage to only work one day a week if that much.

I'm so proud of you for everything you have accomplished and for the awesome person you are. You have so many great qualities that I admire. You have a great personality and are very funny and witty. You always make me laugh. Your sensitivity and kind heart are also a great quality that not many men can say they have and still be a man.

You also have great morals and stick to them and that's something people recognize in you and respect you for. You are one of the most honest people I know. Remember as a kid you could never tell a lie? If we thought you weren't telling the truth, we would ask, "do you promise?" and you would always cave and tell us the truth.

It was so much fun watching you at your Frisbee tournament last weekend. You did a great job playing and being captain of the team. I know it was a hard year to be captain since you had a young team and the freshmen felt entitled to get more playing time. You handled it well and I know you were an awesome captain for the team. I hope you continue to be a leader on the team your senior year and remember to enjoy it.

Your college career is almost to an end. You will be entering the real world soon, but I know whatever you do after college you will succeed and be great at what you do. Keep in mind you may have to work more than one day a week though. Once again, I'm so proud of you and the person you have become. Love you!

Love,
Jaime
(your favorite sister)
(26 years old)

Jonathan,

Happy ½ 70ᵗʰ birthday! Juuuuust kidding. But really, how cool is it that we got to come to Colorado as a family and help celebrate your birthday with you? It' been a blast getting to hang out this week and I definitely think Mom and Dad should secure a place up here so we can do it more often.

This past month has been crazy for both of us with my whole house situation, but it's also been a lot of fun getting to be your client and watching you work. You seriously did an amazing job and I felt completely taken care of throughout the process. Thank you for doing whatever was needed to make this happen for me, I know it wasn't easy! I'm confident that you are the only agent that could have pulled this off and I appreciate you fighting for me throughout the process.

This season was just a reflection of how you've always been to me as an older brother. No matter what, I always knew you would be there for me if I needed you and you never hesitated to help. I definitely feel blessed to have you as my older brother, especially when I look at my friends and see how different their relationships are. Thank you for always being present in my life and desiring to have a relationship with me—I am beyond grateful.

I know these last few months have been a trial for you in many ways, but I'm proud of the way you've faced everything during this time. I am so happy to hear that you took a leap of faith and joined that men's group at church and have been becoming more involved in Gateway. Whether it's that group or another, I hope you continue to seek in that way because God designed us for community—we can't do it all alone. Like we discussed at dinner the other night, God clearly has something special planned for your life, and I can't wait to see how He reveals that as you continue to trust in Him and seek His ways.

Just remember to trust your instinct, not be afraid of the unconventional decision (which has never been a problem for you) and trust that no matter what happens, God will work it together for your good and His glory if you love and seek Him. I'll be here for you no matter what happens with your job(s), relationships, etc. and you'll always have a place to stay in College Station (God's Country).

Love you man!
Vinnie
(25 years old)

Happy Birthday Jaime!!!

Hey little sis, happy 25th birthday! Welcome to the age of lower insurance, your mid- twenties and a slower metabolism!! Yay!! j/k! 25 is a great age and you are in the prime of your life! I am so proud of you and all that you have accomplished lately. You are such a sweet, fun, wholesome individual that I am proud to call my sister. I am really glad that we are so far past sibling rivalry and are now best of friends...that means the world to me.

I really enjoy hanging out with you and just laughing about everything. You crack me up sis! Congratulations again on a wonderful marriage to a wonderful man and two beautiful hairy kids. (dogs) You can see the happiness in your eyes and we are all so happy for ya'll too. Your house looks incredible. You guys really have a lot going for you right now so enjoy it! Good luck on your MS 150 bike race next month.

I never cease to be amazed and impressed by your ability to continually challenge yourself physically and mentally. I'm sure you will do great like you did on your first triathlon too. And as always, I'll be there to cheer you and Caleb on. Break a leg!! Jaime, I love you dearly and again Happy Birthday!

Jonathan
(27 years old)

Jonathan,

I can't believe you're actually 19 years old. That's insane! But I guess it's pretty cool. And the fact that you're going off to college just blows my mind away. It still hasn't hit me yet that you won't be around anymore. It's gonna be so weird without you here. I can honestly say that I'm going to miss you. But I'm so glad that we had the chance to get closer to each other.

I really feel like I can talk to you now, and I mean, you're not only like a brother to me anymore, I consider you a friend also. I mean come on, you should feel honored to be a friend of Jaime Ronca's. Just kidding! But I do feel honored to have you as a friend as well as a brother. Well

I hope you have an awesome time in college and try not to forget about us little people down in Houston.

Love ya Big Bro,
Jaime
(16 years old)

HAPPY BIRTHDAY JONATHAN!!!

Well, well, well....I can't believe you are turning 36!! You sure are getting close to 40. But let's not talk about that depressing fact haha, let's talk about how awesome you are. To start with you have always been a great brother and I consider myself blessed to have you in my life. Well maybe the first few years could have been better, but you helped toughen me up for my sports days. So, thank you.

But really, once we hit high school, I knew you cared about me and had my back and that means the world to me. As we all know, you, Vinnie and I have a unique sibling relationship and I wouldn't trade it for anything. We are family, and I know we will be close forever. I hope you know you are a special person. I've always envied your outgoing personality and zest for life. I don't think you've ever met a stranger. You love being around people, in the middle of the action and thrive in social settings.

And on top of all that you have a desire to help people and make the world a better place. You have such a good heart and have compassion for others. Your fun-loving personality will make you a great dad one day, as it's already made you a great uncle. Our kids, Kellan especially absolutely adores you. He was so excited to hear we were coming to Austin to visit you. Praying for a successful year for you all around. I love you so much and love our relationship.

Love,
Jaime
(33 years old)

Happy Birthday Dad!

Here's an oldie but goodie: Knock Knock, Who's There? Michael. Michael who? Michael Ronca, the Greatest Father in the World!!! Ha ha, but seriously you are truly something special. I appreciate so much that we can always talk so openly about so many topics of life.

It's great to know that I can come to you with my ideas, victories, failures questions and concerns and can always get your advice and honest feedback. It means a lot to me especially as it relates to the big topics of life such as God, love, family and career. Always know that what you and Mom say to me is received with love and it sinks deep for me to process.

I'm very excited to get my new project "Love On" going strong this year and thank you in advance for your love, support and great advice as I grow. I will need it!! Thank you for always being a strong father figure who dedicates himself to work and prayer to provide for his family. It's because of you that we are abundant in finances and spirit. I appreciate all of your previous and current hard work because I know it is very overwhelming at times.

I want to give you a gift. The gift is one I have recently finally accepted. It is that you are fully loved by God and all of us, especially yourself, no matter how hard you work and how successful you become. You and I tend to overwork and we need to remember to love ourselves, give ourselves grace and forgiveness, peace and rest. Keep that in the forefront of your heart and practice it daily. Also remember that God is our ultimate foundation in Protection, Pleasure and Purpose. It's not anything else like money, fame or material possessions because they can't satisfy our eternal longing.

Living these principals each day would make this potentially more stressful season a more pleasurable experience. I know you've got this, Dad! All in all, thank you for being awesome! You and Mom are so generous and loving. I love to see how you walk in your faith and give your time, energy and money to so many causes.

You are blessed abundantly by doing these things. Oh, and thank you for your time and talents over 33 years ago for making your life's masterpiece…ME! LOL!! Dad,

I love you and I'm always here if you need to talk, hang out, or vent. Come visit me more, it's fun in Austin!

Love On,
Jonathan
(33 years old)

Dear Caleb,

Happy Father's Day! Your first of many as you are not only celebrated by us, but your many children that are yet to be born (hint-hint). I am sure as a young man you could only dream of what it was like to be a father and how you would handle the challenges and the joys of such a moment in your life.

Well, I would like to honor you and let you know that you have so impressed me and touched my heart as I watch you father Kellan. When he smiles back at you, I sense the love that he already has for you. I can so see the two of you working in the yard and looking for turtles and all the birds in the trees. You will be a hands-on father, showing Kellan the secrets of life and the beauties of nature. Your strength and faithfulness to your family will bless your children and give them great security. They will watch as you love their mommy, and they will learn how to truly love and respect from your being such a wonderful role model.

Caleb, as a mother, I would always dream of who Jaime would marry and my prayer was that he would love God, love Jaime, be a great provider and an amazing father. What can I say but, my prayers have been answered and I love watching and being a part of the family that you and Jaime are building. You are the best son-in-law one could ask for and I love you for who you are and so thankful that you are the one Jaime chose! Happy Father's Day again, and may this be the beginning of many treasured celebrations that will be celebrated in your life.

Love,
Debi,
(Mama #2)

Happy Birthday Daddy!!!!!

Well, another year passes, but this one is extra special because you became a grandpa. I mean Papi this year. You are now the one entering a new stage in life, the grandparent years. And I have a feeling you are going to have a blast spoiling Kellan. I love seeing you interact with him, and how his face lights up when he sees you. You are going to play an important role in his life.

I'm so grateful he will have you to look up to as one of the male role models in his life. Why, you ask? Because you are a man who stands for what he believes in. You have class, integrity and morals and others respect you for that. You are intelligent, kind and sensitive, and have many years (59 to be exact) of wisdom to share. And you know I think you're the smartest man in the world. But of course, I know, behind every great man is a great mother (that's you grandma).

I wanted to give you a shout out since you gave birth to this man on this day, 59 years ago. I think you are an incredibly amazing, strong woman who I look up to. You never cease to amaze me. Thank you for doing such a great job raising my dad, so he was able to be an amazing father and now grandfather. Happy Birthday Dad!! I love you with all my heart.

Love,
Jaime
(28 years old)

Dearest Mother,

HAPPY MOTHER'S DAY!! Another year gone, and another outstanding performance by you as the best Mom in the Universe. Actually, ask Jonathan or Dad if Coast to Coast has a larger term I could use to describe your greatness. Best mom in the quantum molecular galaxy to the tenth power? Anyway, I guess that's the point.

There really are no words to describe how great of a mom you have been and continue to be. I still remember being the kid in school with the coolest mom. All of the other kids in my class actually had to have their projects done on the due date! Not me. It always seemed that I was sick the day my projects were due, or at the least got to come to school late. Thanks Mom! Not only that, but you helped me complete all of them.

You also taught me the importance of prayer when we only had one quarter left and needed to get that dinosaur out of the vending machine. You've done a great job of sprinkling in lessons of faith throughout events in our childhood. I miss the days of coming home from school and having a gourmet snack waiting for me. Can we start implementing that again now that I'll be living at home?

One of the many things I love about you mom, is how you make everything a special and memorable event. Sometimes I tend to rush things or pass moments up, but you do a great job of making us step back and take in the surroundings. I know you're going to make my graduation a party to remember and can't thank you enough. You deserve this day this year more than any, because of how great you were with helping Grandma through that tough time. As you always do, you sacrificed everything for the good of someone else and helped ease her through the sickness.

I know none of that would have been possible had you not been up there on the East coast for her. It was purely an act of love, and that is exactly what comes to mind when I think of you: Love. Thank you so much for being you, and I can't wait to party in New York! Happy Mother's Day,

Love,
Vinnie .
(21 years old)

Dear Michael,

Wow…how many Father's Days have we celebrated together? 30? Isn't it crazy to see how much time has gone by? I am thrilled that we are able to celebrate you over and over each year, because you so richly deserve the accolades. I know for a fact that our children are who they are because of the consistent love you have shown them since they were born. You never turned away or withheld your love, even in the most trying of times, our children knew they were loved and they had a safe place with you.

Your love for the Lord has been a catalyst for them to find God at such an early age. They felt your strength and commitment to them and have been able to grow up to be amazing young adults, building their own futures with the confidence you gave them as a father. You would always have a way of bringing out the best in each one of our children, not accepting less, but pointing them towards greatness in a strength mixed with love that would give them the desire to grow and mature. Your reward is that your children adore you, want to spend time with you and love to just sit and laugh and share the joys of life together.

You are a blessed man, and I am truly blessed to have a husband who loves so deeply, richly and with a love that is life-changing. Now, my dear, it is time for another season in your life to find those young men who don't have a good father image, and begin to sow into their lives, with the same wisdom you shared with your children, and the same love that God has given you to share. Your input brings an impactful change, and God is saying…it's time…they need you! Happy Father's Day to an amazing father, mentor and husband. We are all changed because of your love for us!!!

Love,
Debi

Happy Mother's Day, Momma!!

Here's something special that flowed out of me today for you:

> *It's about time we get to rhyme*
> *all about the love you've always shined*
> *into the hearts and our growing minds*
> *to remind us that we're born divine!*

As sons and daughters of the Lord
we are here to thrive and have peace of mind.
You see a Mother's job is not so well defined,
but it's the most important job that you'll ever find.

So I'll never take Mother's Day lightly now
and Mom you're the best so take a bow!
Take a seat and hear us shout
all of your praises so that you'll never doubt,
that we do appreciate all that you give,
how you fed us, and clothed us and taught us to live.

That I appreciate all of your energy and time
that you took to cultivate our hearts and minds.
Because it truly helped me see the light and to never be
blind
to the unfortunate plight of the those in need in my life.
The years have passed and now we've matured
and because of you Mom, we serve the Lord.

We bless those around us and share our light,
helping those less fortunate fight the good fight.
And when we take a moment to remember why
we have all of this love planted deep inside
we quickly get wise and realize
that the reason our hearts are double the size
is because our Mom poured her love inside!

Cheers to none other than my gorgeous,
loving Mother, Debi!

Mom, I love you so much! I wrote that rhyme just for you today. I've never really done that before but it just poured out of me with so much love for you today. Mom I am so blessed to have you as my Mother! I truly am the luckiest guy in the world! You have always been there for me and loved unconditionally. I can truly say it is so!
Thank you for being the beating heart and spiritual gangster of the family too, Lol. It means the world growing up in a Godly family and knowing your Mom always has your back. Mom, I am so proud of you too! You made your dreams come true and you have pressed on during the tough times of learning your new craft as a life coach. I love how God is bringing the right people of influence into your path now and He is saying to you, "Debi, I know your heart and I still have much for you to do for my Kingdom"!

I pray you see how amazing of a coach you already are naturally and enjoy the ride! Enjoy yourself in Europe and please come back to Austin afterwards to hang out with me!

Love always,
Jonathan
(37 years old)

Dear Debi,

Debi, glücklich zum Muttertag! Du bist der Beste. Ohne Sie und Ihre Liebe hätten wir keine Familie. Sie sind das Bindeglied, das uns alle zusammenhält. Ihre Liebe, Güte und Ermutigung bringt uns an diesen Ort heute "you zu feiern".

Yes, my little beautiful Fraüen, I wrote this in your native German tongue.

Translation – Debi, Happy Mother's Day! You are the best. Without you and your love we would have no family. You are the glue that holds us all together. Your love, kindness and encouragement bring us to this place today to celebrate "you".

Thank you for being a great wife and Mother to our children. Today is a wonderful time to pause and say "thank you" for being an incredible human being. You wonderfully model sacrificial love and the heart of Jesus in the way that you treat our children. You are patient, kind, forgiving, loving, joyful, long suffering and oh, did I mention patient?

The kids and I are amazed at your consistency and willingness to put yourself on the backburner for our happiness. Your sacrificial love is such a powerful virtue that is so often overlooked because you do it so frequently that we take it for granted. The good news—now all of that gooey love can be invested in Kellan and Natalie. Just make sure you have enough left over for your needy boys and husband, LOL.

I am so pleased that you decided to lead the study on the "War Room". You are a prayer warrior and a leader who can help so many other women become strong and mighty in the Lord. We need women and men who pray for their families, community and the nation and know how to fight. The Bible says "For though we live in the world, we do not wage war as the world does. The weapons we fight with are not the weapons of the world.

On the contrary, they have divine power to demolish strongholds. We demolish arguments and every pretension that sets itself up against the knowledge of God, and we take captive every thought to make it obedient to Christ". I believe there will be great testimonies coming from the war room study. I am excited for you as you raise up the next generation of prayer warriors. I love you, and my world would never be the same without you, my love. Happy Mother's Day!

Love,
Michael

about the author

Debi Ronca is an author, coach, speaker and President of Sequoia Coaching. Her passion is to empower people to realize their value and potential and to begin walking it out in their everyday lives. Debi began her formal coaching journey by becoming certified both with The John Maxwell Team and Leader Breakthru. Her core focus with Sequoia Coaching is helping clients find their unique purpose and calling and guide them through life's transitions.

Whether speaking to leaders in the marketplace or bringing inspirational messages at women's events, her desire is to move people to the next level by expanding their confidence, sense of worth and influence.

Debi and Michael, the love of her life and best friend, have been married since 1979. She is the mother of three beautiful adult children which have been the joyful focus and fulfilled purpose of her life. This new season of being Nana to her grandchildren has brought even more happiness and fulfillment. Originally from Philadelphia, she now lives in Spring, TX with her family.

work with debi

SPEAKING

Debi is a dynamic and passionate speaker, available for conferences and engagements in the marketplace as well as women's events. The messages she shares are empowering and inspirational and bring forth truth and encouragement.

Some of her topics include:
- Leadership
- Motivation
- Family
- Power of Encouragement
- Navigating the Storm

SEQUOIA COACHING

- Equipping you to go to the next level in your business and personal life.
- Finding clarity and identifying road blocks that hinder your potential.
- Adding strength to the areas where you feel stuck or weak.
- Working through transitions that are purposeful in leading you in a new direction.

For more information, or to contact Debi for your next event, visit:

www.DebiRonca.com

work cited

The Holy Bible, New International Version, NIV
Copyright 1973, 1978, 1984, 2011 by Biblica, Inc.

New American Standard Bible,
Copyright – 1960, 1962, 1963, 1968, 1971, 1972, 1973,
1975, 1977, 1996 by the Lockman Foundation, La Habra,
California

chapter 6

I'M ENGAGED TO DADDY

When our daughter Jaime was about to turn thirteen, it became apparent to my husband, Michael, that this particular letter would carry a weightier purpose than his other letters in the past. This letter would signify and trumpet the arrival of a birthday when every young girl begins to transition into the next season in life of becoming a woman. This letter would be different and he had a special message for her.

A few days before her birthday, we went and purchased an Irish Claddagh ring. This ring has a heart with a crown above it and the heart is being held by two hands, one on each side. We chose a garnet stone to be the center of the heart representing Jaime's birthstone. Michael sat down pondering his thoughts, knowing this letter would be one of the most important letters he would write to his daughter. As I said, there was a message, a father's heart that needed to be penned.

His words would guide her in the years ahead. He began to write to his little girl, once again affirming her for who she was, who God created her to be, her value and personal uniqueness. In his letter, he reminded Jaime of his unconditional love for her and then took it to another level where he told her that he would be the man in her life until she met the young man she would marry one day.

Dear Jaime,

Happy Birthday and congratulations! You are now a "teenager". This means that officially your body, mind and emotions will go through many changes as you grow and mature into womanhood. As such you will find these next few years to be both exciting and difficult. You will experience radical extremes, as one minute you will be happy and feel good and the next you will not like anything about yourself. Just remember this condition is temporary and normal for teenagers.

Also remember that God has made you unique and special. He created you and blessed you with your mind, body and physical appearance. He loves you just the way you are, just as Mommy and I do. The present I bought you this year was selected for this particular occasion. It is an Irish wedding ring meant to be worn with the